**Grade 1**

# Summer Skills
## Daily Activity Workbook

Written by **Shannon Keeley**

Illustrations by **Holli Conger**

An imprint of Sterling Children's Books

FLASH KIDS, STERLING, and the distinctive Sterling logo are registered trademarks of
Sterling Publishing Co., Inc.

Published by Sterling Publishing Co., Inc.
387 Park Avenue South, New York, NY 10016
Text and illustrations © 2007 by Flash Kids
Distributed in Canada by Sterling Publishing
c/o Canadian Manda Group, 165 Dufferin Street
Toronto, Ontario, Canada M6K 3H6
Distributed in the United Kingdom by GMC Distribution Services
Castle Place, 166 High Street, Lewes, East Sussex, England BN7 1XU
Distributed in Australia by Capricorn Link (Australia) Pty. Ltd.
P.O. Box 704, Windsor, NSW 2756, Australia

Sterling ISBN 978-1-4114-3416-5

Manufactured in Canada

Lot #:
2 4 6 8 10 9 7 5 3 1
03/10

For information about custom editions, special sales, premium and
corporate purchases, please contact Sterling Special Sales
Department at 800-805-5489 or specialsales@sterlingpublishing.com.

Cover design and production by Mada Design, Inc.

# DEAR PARENT,

As a parent, you want your child to have time to relax and have fun during the summer, but you don't want your child's math and reading skills to get rusty. How do you make time for summer fun and also ensure that your child will be ready for the next school year?

This *Summer Skills Daily Activity Workbook* provides short, fun activities in reading and math to help children keep their skills fresh all summer long. This book not only reviews what children learned during kindergarten, it also introduces what they'll be learning in first grade. The numbered daily activities make it easy for children to complete one activity a day and stay on track the whole summer long. Best of all, the games, puzzles, and stories help children retain their knowledge as well as build new skills. By the time your child finishes the book, he or she will be ready for a smooth transition into first grade.

As your child completes the activities in this book, shower him or her with encouragement and praise. You can feel good knowing that you are taking an active and important role in your child's education. Helping your child complete the activities in this book is providing him or her with an excellent example—that you value learning, every day! Have a wonderful summer and, most of all, have fun learning together!

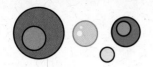 

# BUBBLY B

**b**ed          we**b**

Practice writing the letters **Bb**.

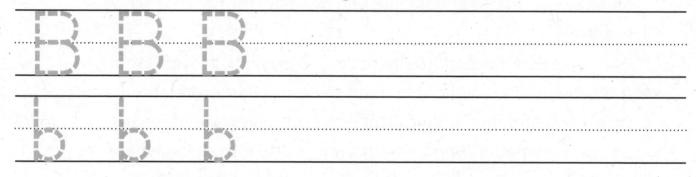

Write **Bb** if the picture **begins** with the **b** sound.

**Beginning B**

_____     _____     _____

Write **Bb** if the picture **ends** with the **b** sound.

**Ending B**

_____     _____     _____

# TWO TULIPS

Connect the numbers **1** through **10** to add tulips to the garden.

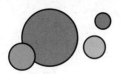
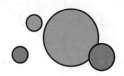

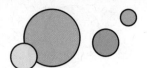
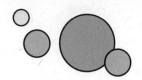

# CARL'S CANDY

**c**at

Practice writing the letters **Cc**.

C    C    C    C

c    c    c

How did Carl get across the pond to his candy?
Color the pictures that begin with the **c** sound.

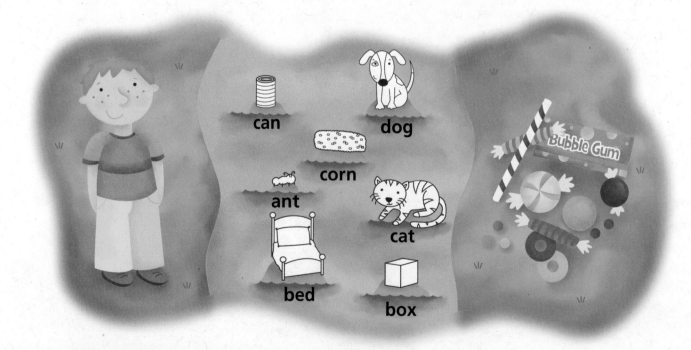

can    dog

corn

ant    cat

bed

box

# NUMBERS FUN

Color the number of boxes for each row. The first one is done for you.

| 2 | | | | | |
|---|---|---|---|---|---|
| 4 | | | | | |
| 1 | | | | | |
| 3 | | | | | |
| 5 | | | | | |

Find the numbers **1**, **2**, **3**, **4**, and **5** and circle them.

| 4 | I | E | S | 5 |
|---|---|---|---|---|
| L | 1 | L | R | 3 |
| C | X | 2 | Q | |

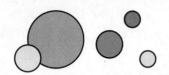
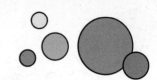

# DOGHOUSE D

**d**og

sa**d**

Practice writing the letters **Dd**.

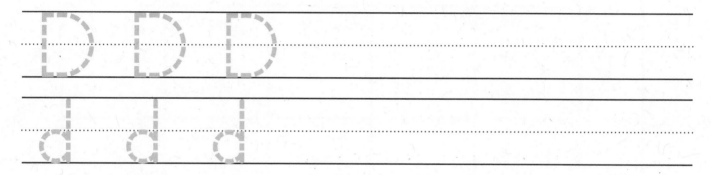

Draw a line from each picture to the correct doghouse.

**Beginning D**

**Ending D**

# BALLOON BUNCHES

Draw balloons to equal the number at the bottom of each bunch.

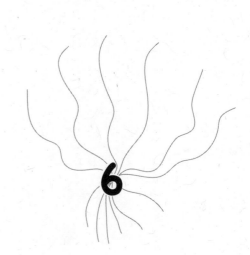

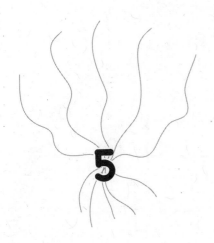

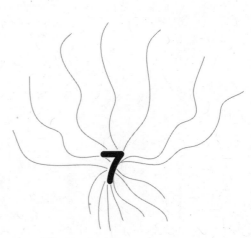

**10**

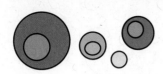
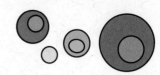

# ALPHABALL

Fill in the missing capital or lowercase letters in **ABC** order.

| ABC |
|-----|
| DEF |
| GHI |
| JKL |
| MNO |
| PQR |
| STU |
| VWX |
| YZ |

A _B_ C D
E __ G H I __
K L M __ O P
__ R S __ U
__ W X
__ Z

| abc |
|-----|
| def |
| ghi |
| jkl |
| mno |
| pqr |
| stu |
| vwx |
| yz |

a b __ d e
f __ h __ j __
l m n __ p q
__ s t u __ w
__ y z

# GET IN SHAPE!

Connect the matching shapes. Write the letter below.

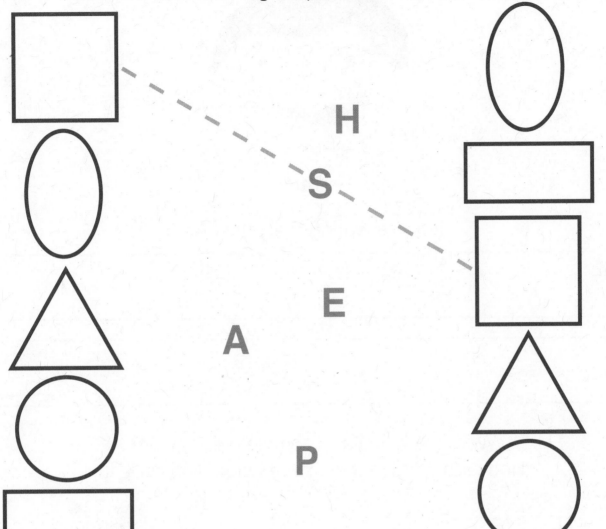

H

S

E

A

P

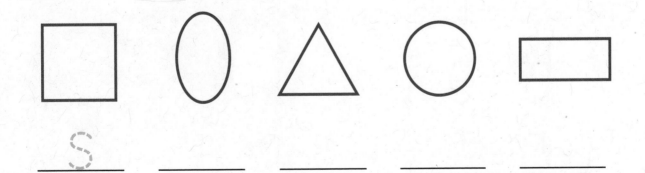

S ___ ___ ___ ___

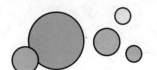
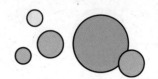

# SHORT A ATTIC

d**a**d

Practice writing the letters **Aa**.

A  A  A

a  a  a

Write the vowel **a** to complete each word.
Find each word in the picture below and circle it.

__nt

c__p

b__g

r__t

# TRAIN OF TEN

Trace the numbers **1–10**.

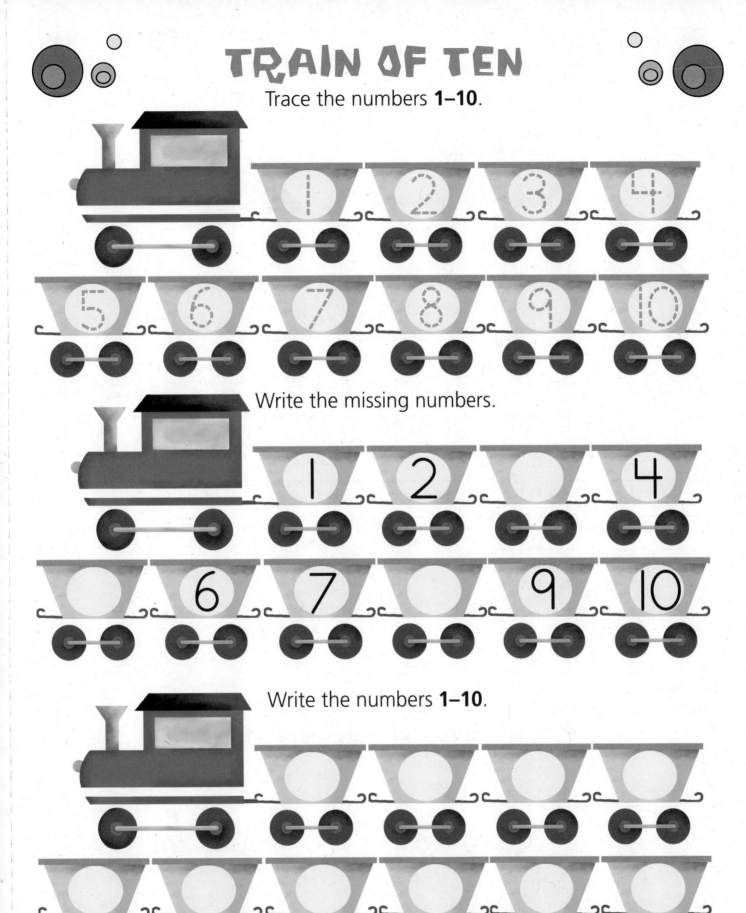

Write the missing numbers.

Write the numbers **1–10**.

# FISH FUN

<u>f</u>ish           roo<u>f</u>

Practice writing the letters **Ff**.

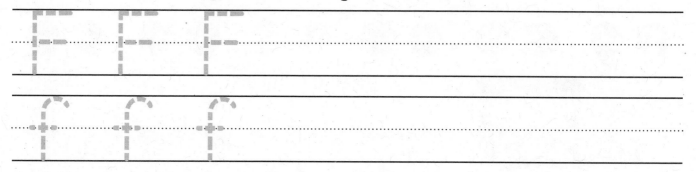

Write **Ff** if the picture **begins** with the **f** sound.

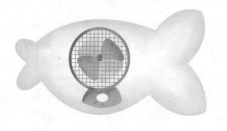

Beginning F  _____   _____   _____

Write **Ff** if the picture **ends** with the **f** sound.

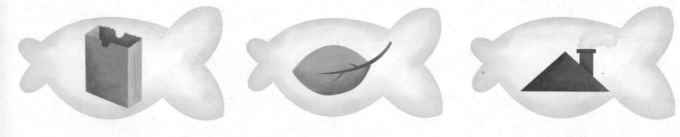

_____   _____   _____                    Ending F

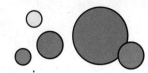

# HOT DOTS

Connect the numbers **1** through **25** to find a sunny surprise.

# GOLDFISH GAME

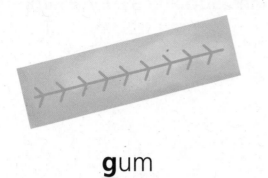

**g**um

bu**g**

Practice writing the letters **Gg**.

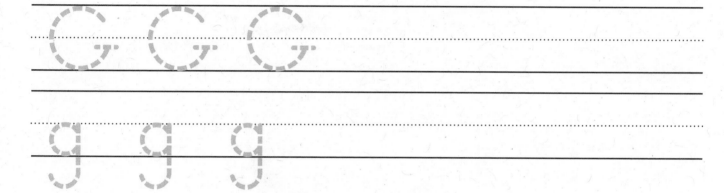

Draw a line from each picture to the correct fish bowl.

**Beginning G**

**Ending G**

**Day 13:
Beginning G**

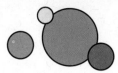

# SUPER SIZES

Circle the picture that is **bigger** than the first one in the row.

Circle the picture that is **smaller** than the first one in the row.

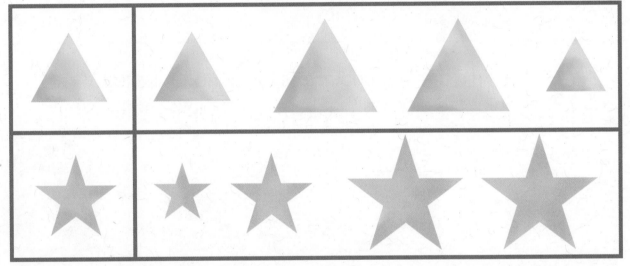

Circle the picture that is the **same size** as the first one in the row.

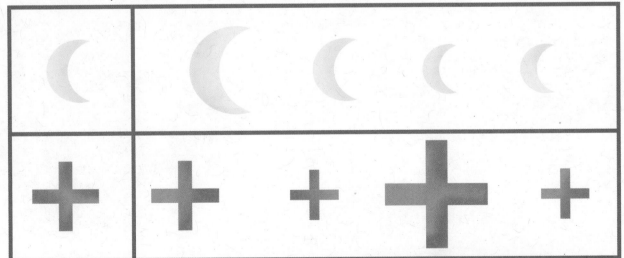

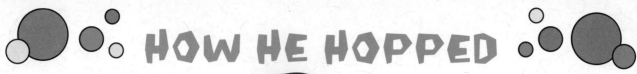

**h**ug

Practice writing the letters **Hh**.

How did the frog hop across the pond to the log?
Color the pictures that begin with the **h** sound.

# BOXES OF BALLOONS

Circle the group with **more** balloons.

Circle the group with **less** balloons

Draw a line to match the letter pairs **Aa** through **Zz**.

Day 17:
Letter Pairs

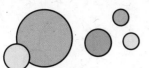 # COIN CONNECTION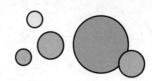

Connect the matching coins. Write how much each is worth below.

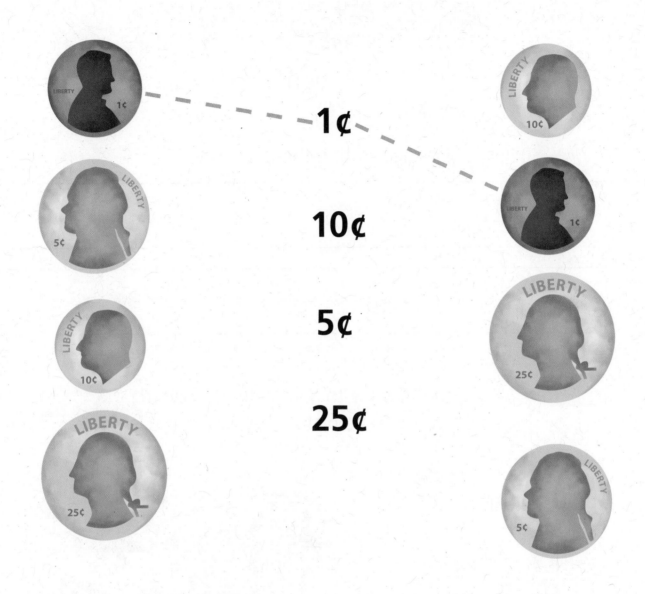

1¢

10¢

5¢

25¢

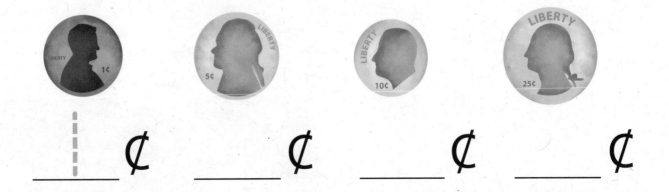

_____ ¢   _____ ¢   _____ ¢   _____ ¢

p<u>e</u>n

Practice writing the letters **Ee**.

E E E

e e e

Write the vowel **e** to complete each word.
Find each word in the picture below and circle it.

h__n

b__ll

__gg

n__t

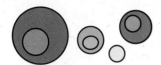
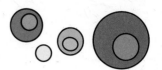

# ZANY TRAINS

Draw the next shape in each pattern.

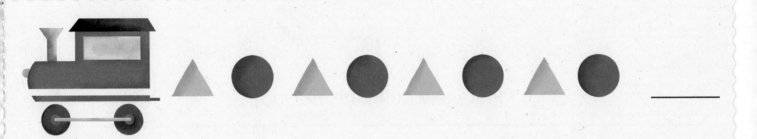

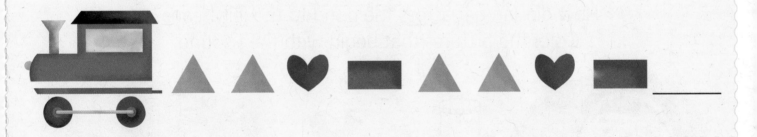

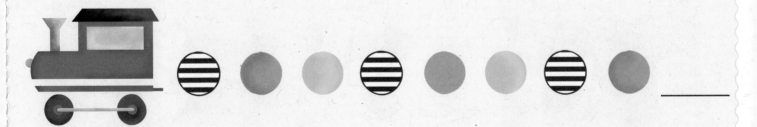

# JELLYBEAN JOURNEY

**j**et

Practice writing the letters **Jj**.

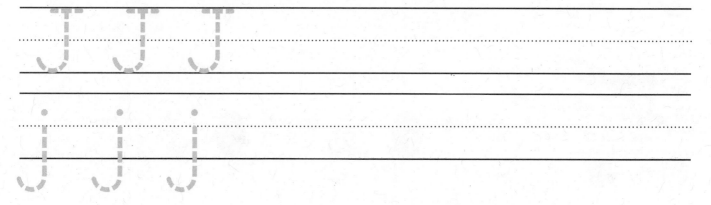

How did Jan get across the pond to the jellybeans?
Color the pictures that begin with the **j** sound.

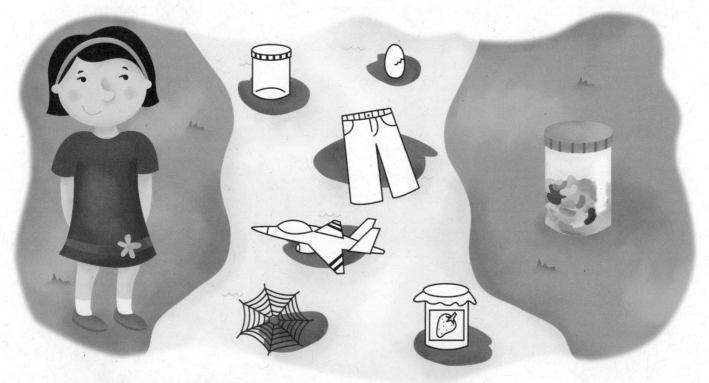

# COLOR CODE

Find two examples of each shape at the beach.
Use the code at the bottom to color the pictures.

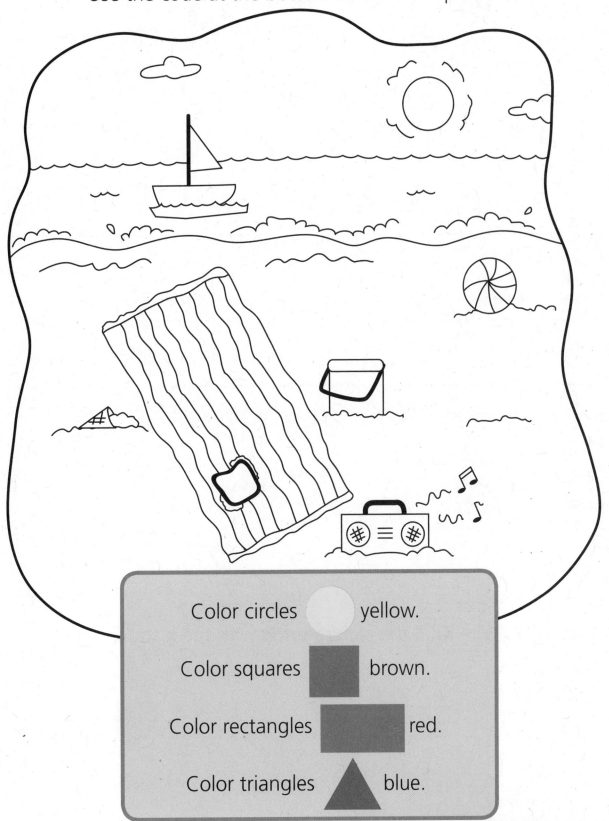

Color circles yellow.

Color squares brown.

Color rectangles red.

Color triangles blue.

# KITE TAILS

**k**ite          lea**k**

Practice writing the letters **Kk**.

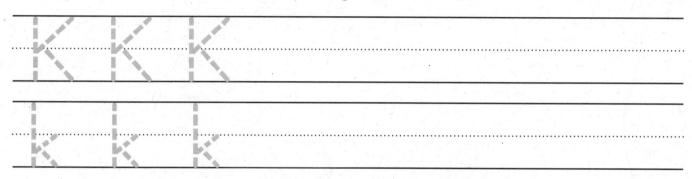

Write **Kk** if the picture **begins** with the **k** sound.

Beginning K

_____  _____  _____

Write **Kk** if the picture **ends** with the **k** sound.

Ending K

_____  _____  _____

# PATTERN POWER

Complete the patterns.

# LEAFY L

<u>l</u>eg                    sea<u>l</u>

## Practice writing the letters **Ll**.

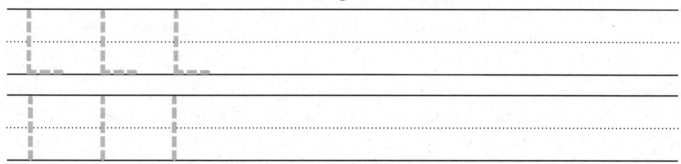

Draw a line from each picture to the correct tree.

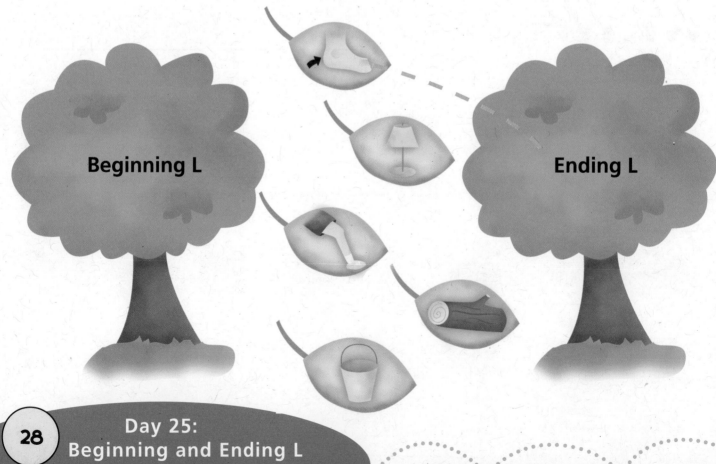

**Beginning L**                    **Ending L**

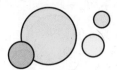
# BALLOON BUDDIES

Draw a line to connect the matching balloon pairs.

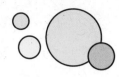

# STORY OUT OF ORDER

Number the boxes to show the order.

**The cat likes Dad.**

**A jar is in the bag.**

**Dad has a bag**

**Jam is on Dad.**

**The cat likes jam, too.**

**Dad likes jam.**

Write a title for the story.

_____

.................................

_____

Match each picture with the correct number.

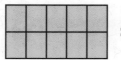 = 10

11

12

13

14

15

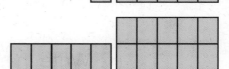
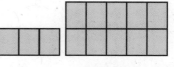
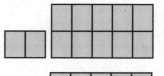
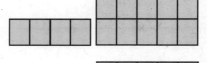

- - - - - - - - - - - - - - - - - - - - - - - - - - - - - - - - - - - - - - - - - - -

11

12

13

14

15

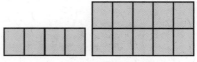
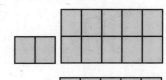
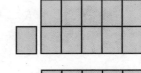
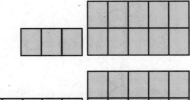
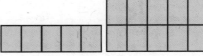

# SHORT I INN

p_in

Practice writing the letters **Ii**.

Write the vowel **i** to complete each word.
Find each word in the picture below and circle it.

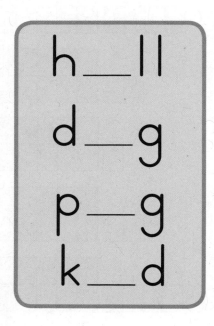

h__ll

d__g

p__g

k__d

Count the cars, then write the number in the engine.

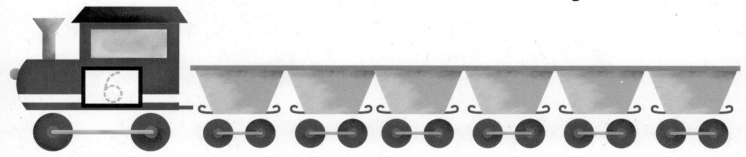

Count the cars, then add one more car to the end.
Write the total in the engine.

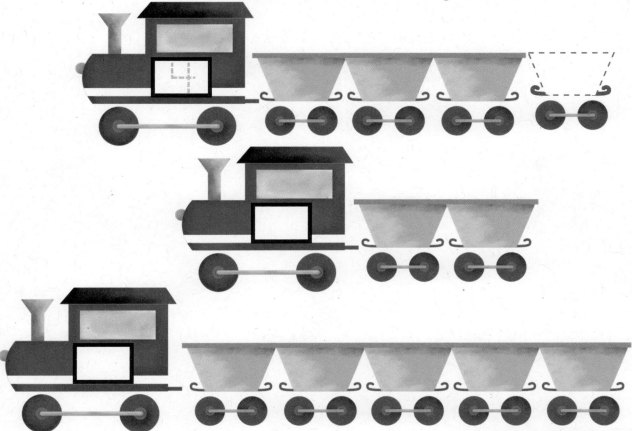

**m**at          ha**m**

Practice writing the letters **Mm**.

M M M

m m m

Draw a line from each picture to the correct mailbox.

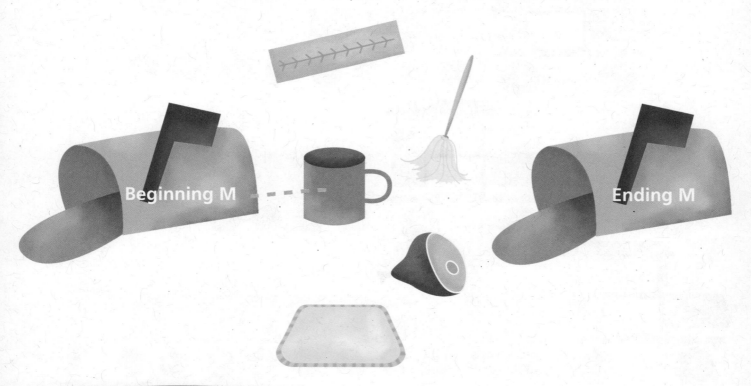

Beginning M          Ending M

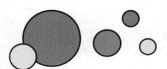 # TAKE YOUR TIME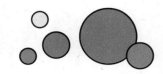

Look at the pictures in each box.
Circle the thing that takes **more** time.

About how long would it take? Circle the answer.

30 seconds    30 minutes

4 minutes          4 hours

2 minutes    2 seconds

**n**ap                    pe**n**

Practice writing the letters **Nn**.

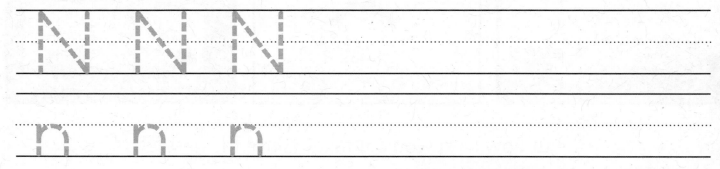

Write **Nn** if the picture **begins** with the **n** sound.

_____   _____   _____

Write **Nn** if the picture **ends** with the **n** sound.

_____   _____

Add the pennies, then write the total.

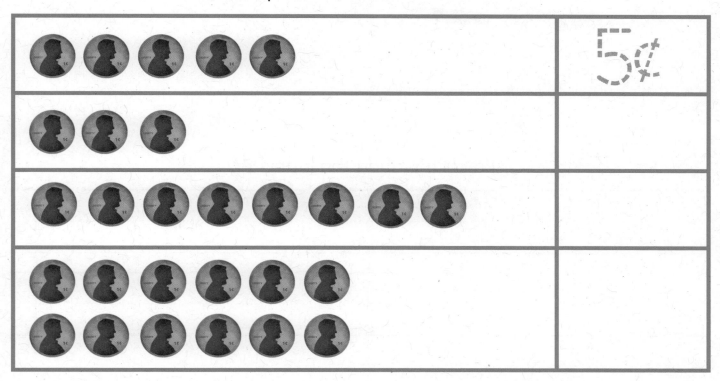

Circle pennies to equal the number on the left.

4¢

7¢

5¢

# PAM'S PATH

**p**ot                         ho**p**

Practice writing the letters **Pp**.

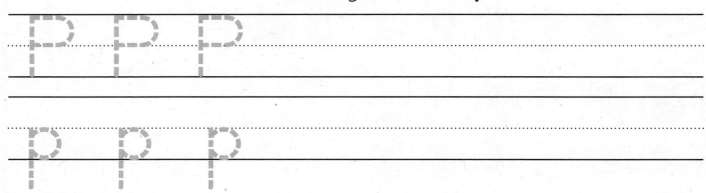

Help Pam get to her prize! Connect the pictures that **begin** with the **p** sound and follow the path. Then connect the pictures that **end** with the **p** sound and follow the path.

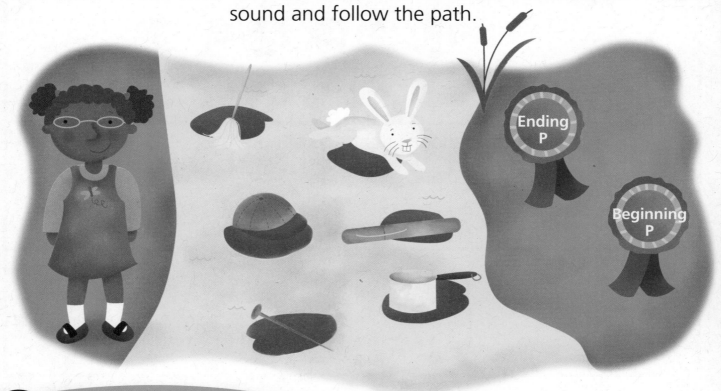

# BYE BYE BALLOON

One balloon floated away from each group.
Count the balloons and subtract.

  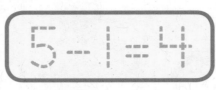

5 – 1 = 4

---

**1.**

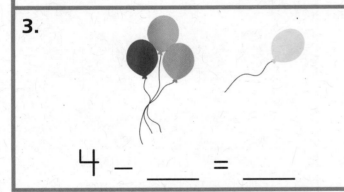

7 – 1 = ___

**2.**

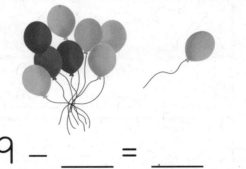

9 – ___ = ___

**3.**

4 – ___ = ___

**4.**

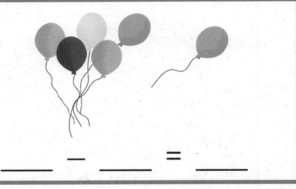

___ – ___ = ___

If all the balloons float away, there are 0 left.

**5.**

2 – 2 = 0

**6.**

3 – 3 = ___

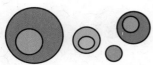

# HIDE AND SEEK

The word on the left is hiding in the sentence.
Circle it each time you see it.

**1.** **you**

**You** go hide.
We will find **you**!

**2.** **not**

Do not come.
We are not ready!

**3.** **in**

What's in the box?
You are not in the box!

**4.** **we**

We are not in that box.
Look where we are.

**5.** **go**

Go look in the box.
Now we can go hide.

Copy the words.

**you** _____

**not** _____

**in** _____

**we** _____

**go** _____

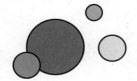

# TIME LINES

Match each clock to the correct time.

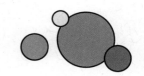

four o'clock          **7:00**

ten o'clock          **12:00**

seven o'clock          **2:00**

two o'clock          **9:00**

twelve o'clock          **4:00**

nine o'clock          **10:00**

t**o**p

Practice writing the letters **Oo**.

Write the vowel **o** to complete each word.
Find each word in the picture below and circle it.

p__t

s__ck

B__b

m__p

Bob

# TAG ALONG TRAIN

More train cars want to tag along.
Add the cars, then write the total in the engine.

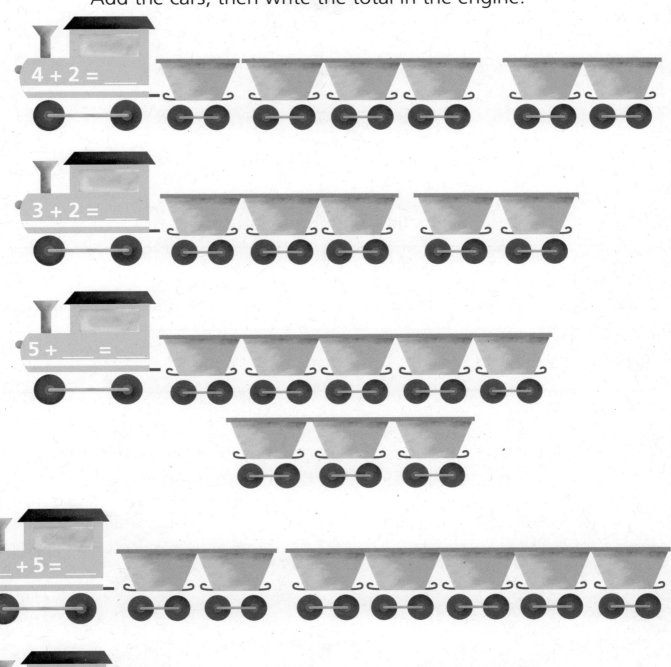

4 + 2 = ____

3 + 2 = ____

5 + ____ = ____

____ + 5 = ____

____ + ____ = ____

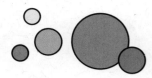

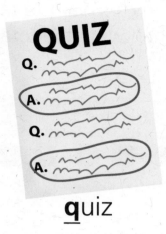

**q**uiz

Practice writing the letters **Qq**.

How did the queen get across the pond to her throne?
Color the pictures that begin with the **q** sound.

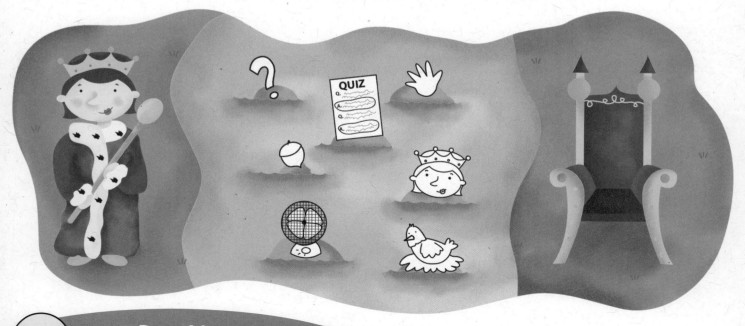

# RACE FOR FIRST PLACE

Look at the picture above.
Draw a line to show which place each runner came in.

| 1st | | Ted |
|-----|--|-----|
| 2nd | | Jen |
| 3rd | | Sam |
| 4th | | Kim |
| 5th | | Val |

Now write the ordinal number next to each runner's name.

**Ted:** _third_

**Jen:** _____

**Sam:** _____

**Val:** _____

**Kim:** _____

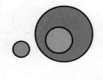

# ROCKET RACE

**r**ug

ca**r**

Practice writing the letters **Rr**.

R R R

r r r

Write **Rr** if the picture **begins** with the **r** sound.

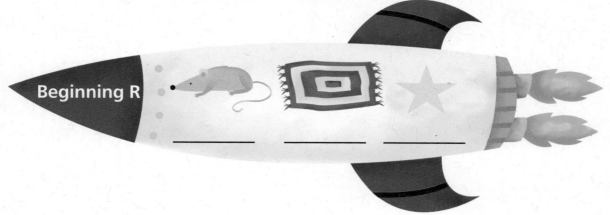

Beginning R

_____  _____  _____

Write **Rr** if the picture **ends** with the **r** sound.

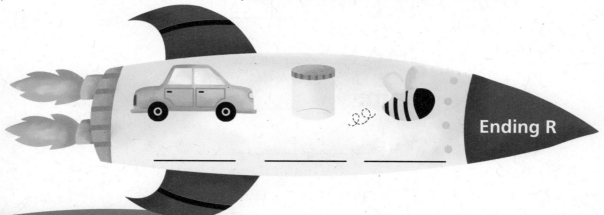

Ending R

_____  _____  _____

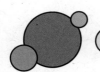 # MADE IN THE SHADE

Shade the squares, then cross out the number to be subtracted. Count how many are left and write the number.

| | | | | | | | | | | |
|---|---|---|---|---|---|---|---|---|---|---|
| 5 − 3 = **2** | ⊠ | ⊠ | ⊠ | ▨ | ▨ | | | | | |
| 7 − 4 = ____ | | | | | | | | | | |
| 6 − 2 = ____ | | | | | | | | | | |
| 4 − 1 = ____ | | | | | | | | | | |
| 3 − 0 = ____ | | | | | | | | | | |
| 8 − 6 = ____ | | | | | | | | | | |
| 2 − 1 = ____ | | | | | | | | | | |
| 5 − 5 = ____ | | | | | | | | | | |
| 10 − 4 = ____ | | | | | | | | | | |

# SOCCER SORT

**s**ub          bu**s**

Practice writing the letters **Ss**.

S  S  S

s  s  s

Draw a line from each ball to the correct goal.

Beginning S          Ending S

# BALLOON CLUES

Add or subtract. Use the balloons as picture clues.

**1.**

$3 + 4 = \underline{7}$

**2.**

$2 + 2 = \underline{\phantom{0}}$

**3.**

$5 + \underline{\phantom{0}} = \underline{\phantom{0}}$

**4.**

$6 - 2 = \underline{4}$

**5.**

$8 - 3 = \underline{\phantom{0}}$

**6.**

$10 - \underline{\phantom{0}} = \underline{\phantom{0}}$

# TWO WORDS TOGETHER

Two words join together to make a compound word.

sun + rise = *sunrise*

Join the two words together and write the compound word.

1.

foot + ball = _____

2.

dog + house = _____

3.

mail + box = _____

4.

ant + hill = _____

5.

gum + ball = _____

50 Day 47: Compound Words

# HALFTIME

Draw a line to connect each picture with its other half.

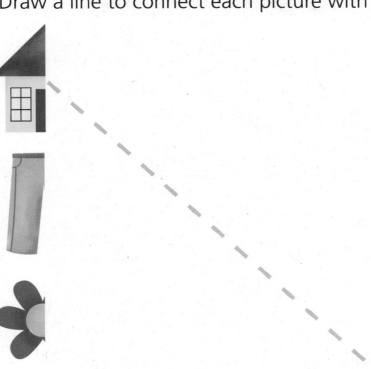

Draw a line to divide each picture in half.

Now draw the other half.

**t_u_b**

Practice writing the letters **Uu**.

Write the vowel **u** to complete each word.
Find each word in the picture below and circle it.

g __ m

b __ s

b __ g

s __ n

# ALL ABOARD ADDITION

Add. Then circle the car whose total matches the
number in the engine.

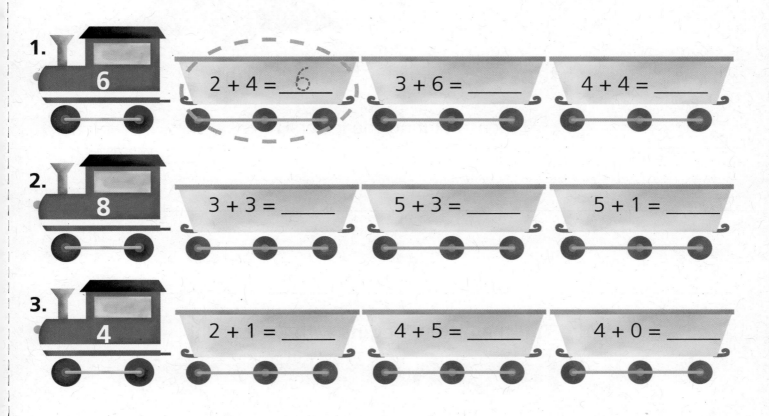

**1.** 6 | 2 + 4 = _6_ | 3 + 6 = _____ | 4 + 4 = _____

**2.** 8 | 3 + 3 = _____ | 5 + 3 = _____ | 5 + 1 = _____

**3.** 4 | 2 + 1 = _____ | 4 + 5 = _____ | 4 + 0 = _____

Fill in the missing number.
Each problem should equal the number in the engine.

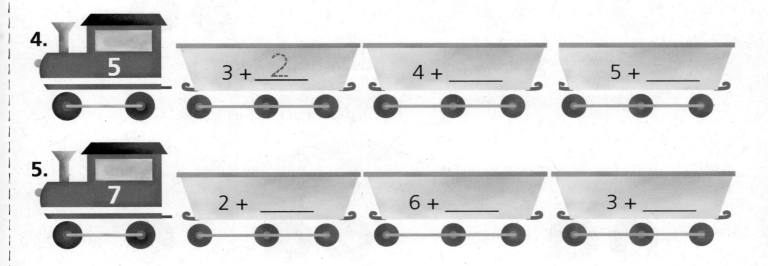

**4.** 5 | 3 + _2_ | 4 + _____ | 5 + _____

**5.** 7 | 2 + _____ | 6 + _____ | 3 + _____

# TRUCKS OF T

**t**op

ba**t**

Practice writing the letters **Tt**.

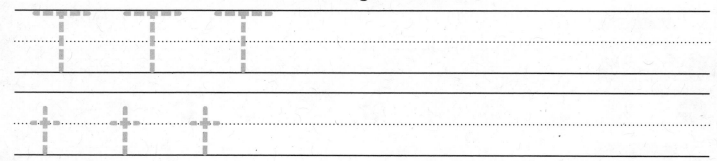

Write **Tt** if the picture **begins** with the **t** sound.

Beginning T

10

Write **Tt** if the picture **ends** with the **t** sound.

Ending T

# NIFTY FIFTY

Connect the numbers **25** through **50** to find a speedy surprise.

**v**an     **w**agon

Practice writing the letters **Vv** and **Ww**.

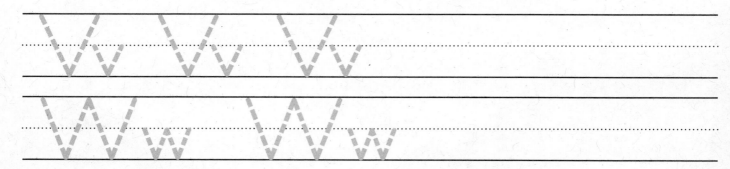

Draw a line from each picture to the correct letter.

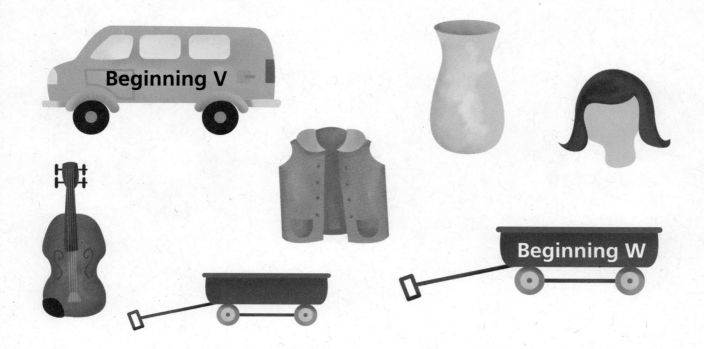

Beginning V

Beginning W

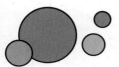
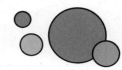

# LOOK CLOSELY!

Circle the picture that is the **same** as the first one in the row.

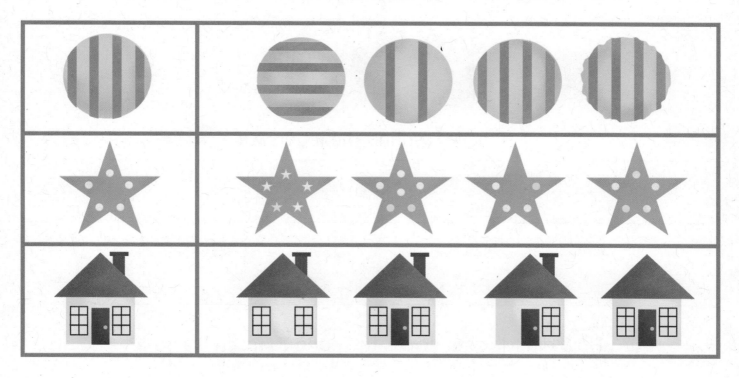

Cross out the picture that is **different** from the first in the row.

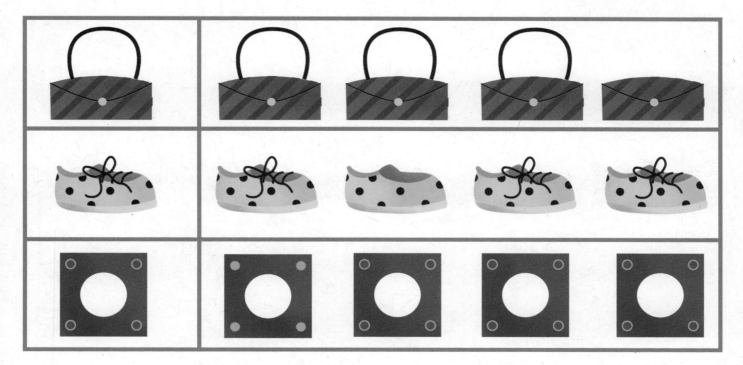

# A BOX FOR MAX

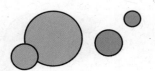
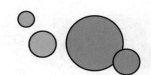

mi**x**

Practice writing the letters **Xx**.

How did Max get across the pond to reach his box?
Color the pictures that end with the **x** sound.

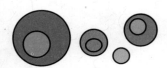 # BALLOON BASICS

## Add or subtract.

**1.**
$$\begin{array}{r} 3 \\ +\ 6 \\ \hline \end{array}$$

**2.**
$$\begin{array}{r} 7 \\ -\ 5 \\ \hline \end{array}$$

**3.**
$$\begin{array}{r} 5 \\ +\ 0 \\ \hline \end{array}$$

**4.**
$$\begin{array}{r} 10 \\ -\ 8 \\ \hline \end{array}$$

**5.**
$$\begin{array}{r} 4 \\ +\ 3 \\ \hline \end{array}$$

**6.**
$$\begin{array}{r} 6 \\ -\ 5 \\ \hline \end{array}$$

**7.**
$$\begin{array}{r} 8 \\ +\ 1 \\ \hline \end{array}$$

**8.**
$$\begin{array}{r} 9 \\ -\ 9 \\ \hline \end{array}$$

**9.**
$$\begin{array}{r} 3 \\ +\ 7 \\ \hline \end{array}$$

**10.**
$$\begin{array}{r} 10 \\ +\ 5 \\ \hline \end{array}$$

**11.**
$$\begin{array}{r} 4 \\ +\ 4 \\ \hline \end{array}$$

**12.**
$$\begin{array}{r} 1 \\ -\ 0 \\ \hline \end{array}$$

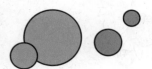
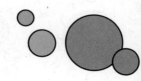

# Y VERSUS Z

**y**awn          **z**ip

Practice writing the letters **Yy** and **Zz**.

Draw a line to connect each picture with the correct letter.

Beginning Y

O

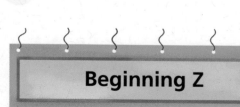

Beginning Z

# MATH MATCH

Solve each problem.
Draw a line to connect the problems that have the same answer.

$3 + 3 =$ ___6___

$4 - 2 =$ ___

$1 + 8 =$ ___

$7 - 2 =$ ___

$3 + 5 =$ ___

$6 - 3 =$ ___

$3 - 0 =$ ___

$8 + 0 =$ ___

$8 - 6 =$ ___

$6 + 3 =$ ___

$10 - 4 =$ ___6___

$4 + 1 =$ ___

# RHYME TIME

Draw a line to match the pictures whose names rhyme.

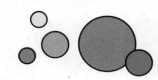

Complete the rhyming words.

__m__ug     ___ug     ___ ___g     ___ ___ ___

__r__at     ___at     ___ ___t     ___ ___ ___

**Day 59:
Rhyming**

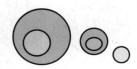 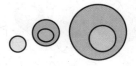

# STAY ON TRACK!

Count by 5s and write the missing numbers.

1. | 5 | 10 | 15 | 20 | _____ |

2. | 30 | _____ | 40 | _____ | 50 |

3. | | 10 | | | 25 |

4. | _____ | 35 | _____ | 45 | _____ |

# PENCIL PALS

## Circle the correct word.

box
fox

bell
bed

fork
fan

cat
hat

## Fill in the missing letters. Use the letters on the left to help.

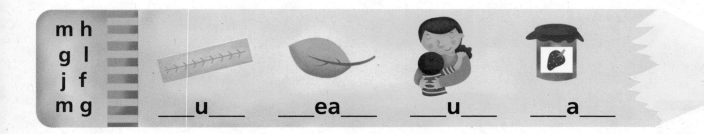

m h
g l
j f
m g

___u___     ___ea___     ___u___     ___a___

## Write the name of each picture. Use the words on the left to help.

dog
cab
ham
log

_____  _____  _____  _____

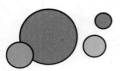
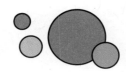

# IT'S A DATE

Number the days on the calendar 1–30.

## June

| Sunday | Monday | Tuesday | Wednesday | Thursday | Friday | Saturday |
|--------|--------|---------|-----------|----------|--------|----------|
|        |        | 1       |           |          |        |          |
|        |        |         |           |          |        |          |
|        |        |         |           |          |        |          |
|        |        |         |           |          |        |          |
|        |        |         |           |          |        |          |

Look at the calendar to answer the questions or follow the directions.

**1.** What month is the calendar for? _____

**2.** Circle the days of the week.

**3.** How many days are in a week? _____

**4.** Draw a star on the last day of the month.

**5.** How many Saturdays are in June? _____

**Bonus Question:**

What month is your birthday? _____

Day 62:
Calendar Skills

65

# WRAPPING UP

Circle the correct word.

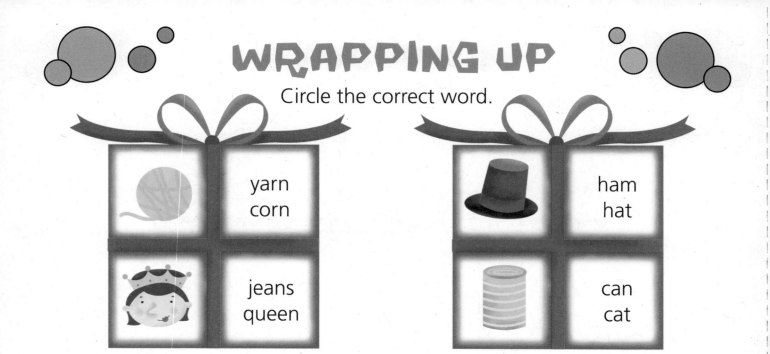

yarn
corn

jeans
queen

ham
hat

can
cat

Fill in the missing letters. Use the letters in the middle to help.

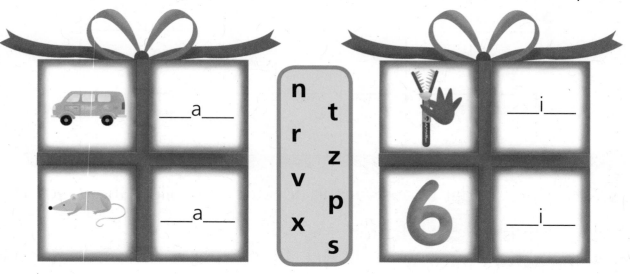

___a___

___a___

n
r
v
x

t
z
p
s

___i___

6   ___i___

Write the name of each picture. Use the words on the left to help.

quiz
web
sun
vase

_____   _____   _____   _____

# COPY CATS

Copy each pattern in the boxes below.

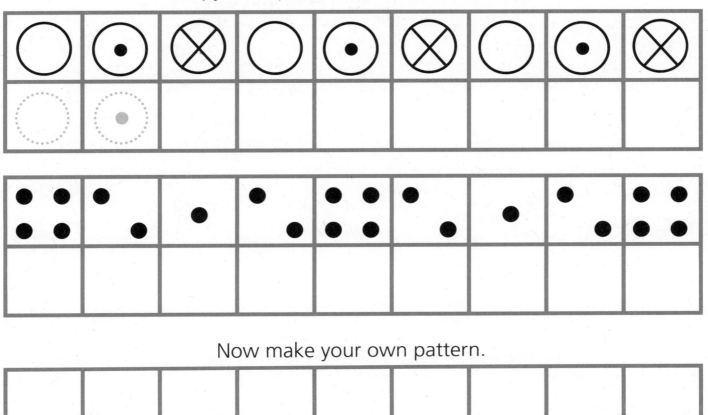

Now make your own pattern.

Copy the picture. Use the dots to help.

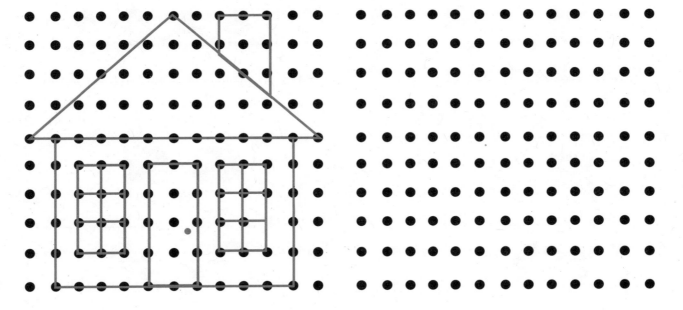

# MORE THAN ONE

To show there is more than one, add **s** at the end.

| **Singular** | **Plural** |
|---|---|
| bed | bed + s = beds |

Add **s** and write the plural of each word.

**1.**

bell     **bells**

**2.**

key    ___ ___ ___ ___

Write the singular and the plural of each word.

**3.**

___ ___ ___    ___ ___ ___

**4.**

___ ___ ___ ___    ___ ___ ___ ___

Sometimes you add **es** to show there is more than one. Write the plurals.

**5.**

___ ___ ___    ___ ___ ___

**6.**

___ ___ ___    ___ ___ ___

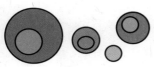 # BALLOON BLUES

If the number and the word on the balloon match, color it blue.
If they don't match, cross it out.

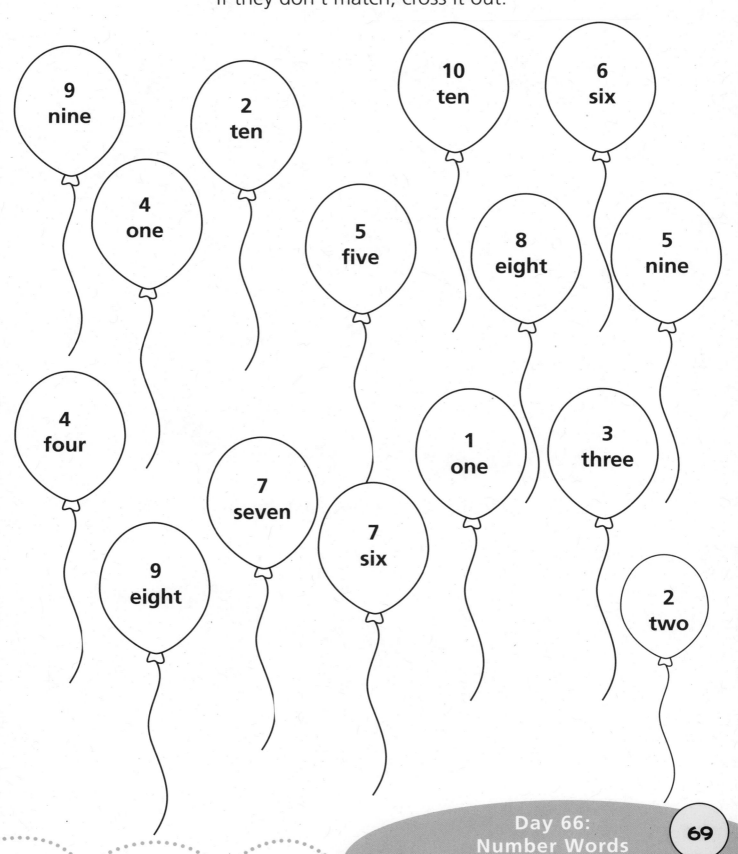

9
nine

2
ten

4
one

10
ten

6
six

5
five

8
eight

5
nine

4
four

1
one

3
three

7
seven

7
six

2
two

9
eight

## Circle the picture that shows what happened before.

**1. a)**    **b)**    **c)**

## Circle the picture that shows what happened after.

**2. a)**    **b)**    **c)**

# THE PRICE IS RIGHT

Look at the price for each item.
Draw a line to the group of nickels that matches the price.

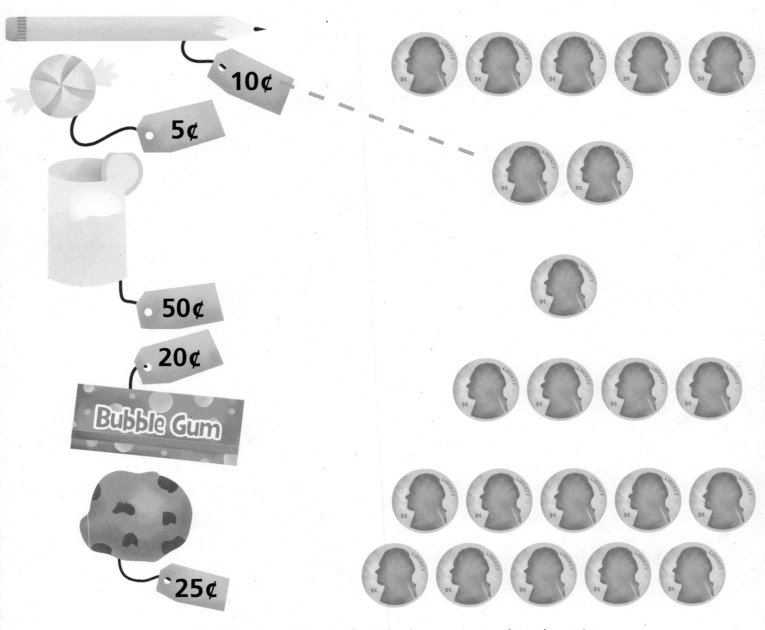

10¢

5¢

50¢

20¢

Bubble Gum

25¢

Circle the number of nickels you need to buy it.

40¢

# READY, SET, REVIEW!

Circle the word or write the letters to name each picture.
Each time you hear a short vowel sound, that vowel scores a point. See which vowel wins the race!

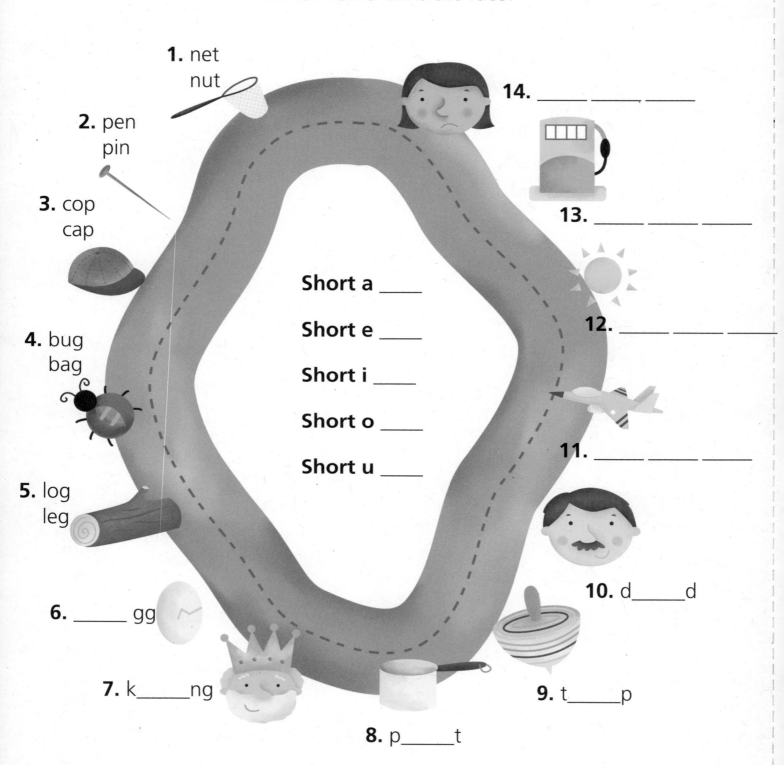

**1.** net
nut

**2.** pen
pin

**3.** cop
cap

**4.** bug
bag

**5.** log
leg

**6.** _____ gg

**7.** k_____ng

**8.** p_____t

**9.** t_____p

**10.** d_____d

**11.** _____ _____ _____

**12.** _____ _____ _____

**13.** _____ _____ _____

**14.** _____ _____ _____

Short a _____

Short e _____

Short i _____

Short o _____

Short u _____

Day 69:
Review a, e, i, o, u

# TRAINS ON TIME

The trains were supposed to arrive at 3:00.
Connect each train with the time it arrived.

**1.**
One hour late

**a) 2:00**

**2.**
One hour early

**b) 5:00**

**3.**
On time

**c) 3:00**

**4.**
Two hours late

**d) 4:00**

Now draw the hands on each clock to show the time.

10:00

7:00

2:00

12:00

4:00

Fill in the letters that make the **long a** sound.

**1.**

**a_e**

l__k___   v___s___   g___m___   t___p___

**2.**

**ai**

p___ ___l   r___ ___n   m___ ___l   m___ ___d

**3.**

**ay**

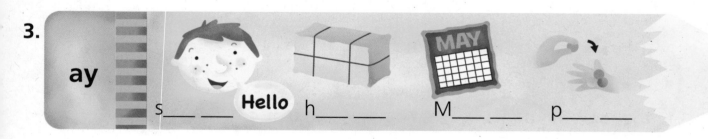

s___ ___   h___ ___   M___ ___   p___ ___

Connect the numbers **75** through **100** to see what's hopping.

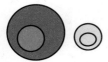

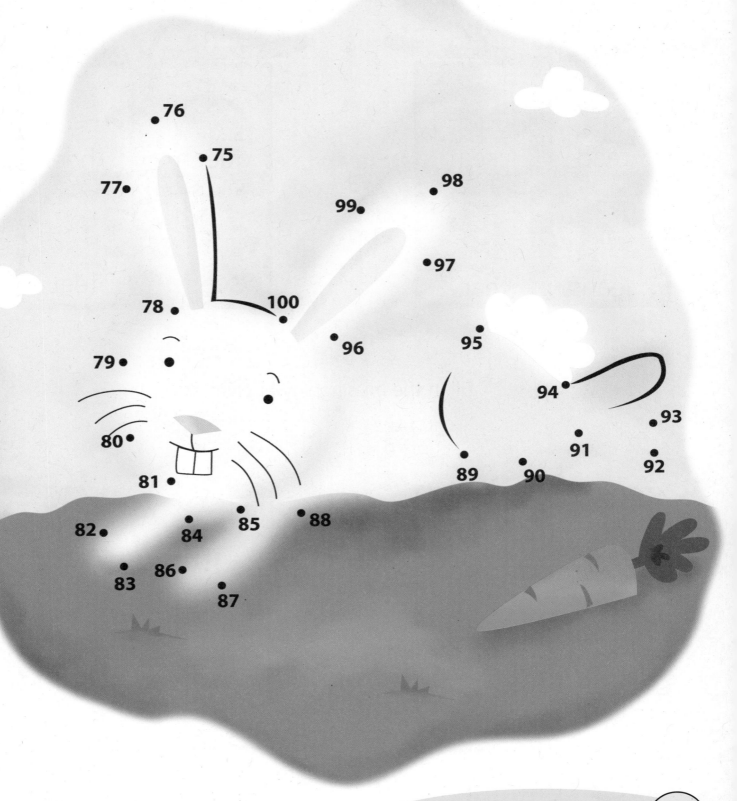

# LONG VOWEL E

Circle the vowel pair in each word.

**1.**

read
seal
jeans
ear

**2.**

queen
heel
see
feet

Fill in the missing vowel pairs.

ea

**3.**

l__ __f
t__ __
l__ __k
b__ __k

ee

**4.**

b__ __
j__ __p
tr__ __
s__ __d

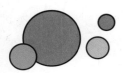
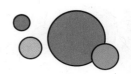

# TERRIFIC TEENS

Trace the numbers and count by 10s.

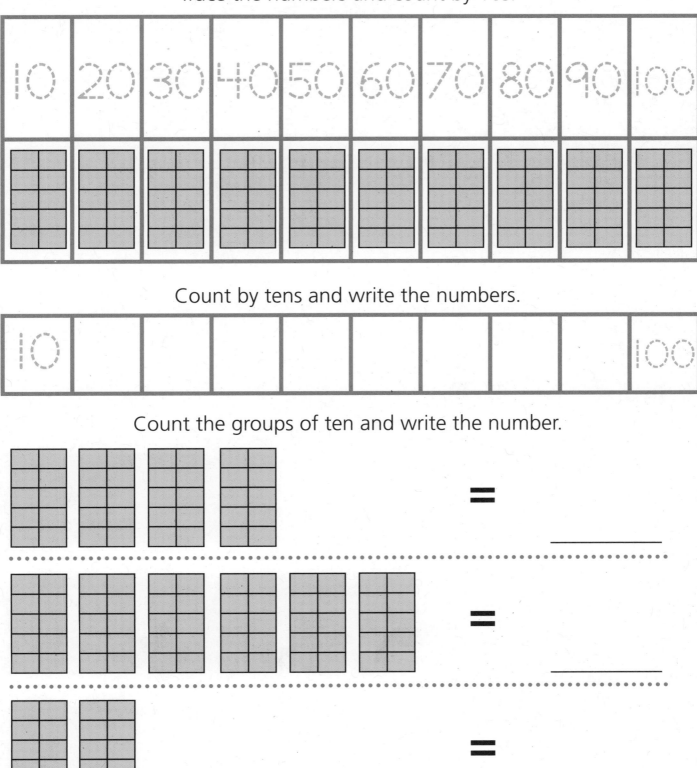

Count by tens and write the numbers.

Count the groups of ten and write the number.

=  _____

=  _____

=  _____

# LONG VOWEL I

Fill in the letters that make the **long i** sound.

**1.**

**i_e**

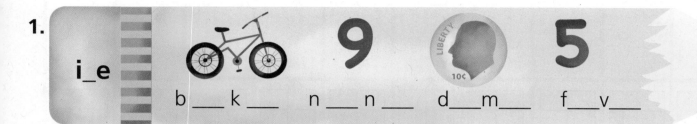

b___k___    n___n___    d___m___    f___v___

**2.**

**ie**

t___ ___    p___ ___

**3.**

**y**

fl___    cr___    sk___    dr___

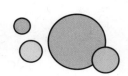

# BEAUTIFUL BALLOONS

Shade the boxes in the graph to show how many
of each type of balloon.

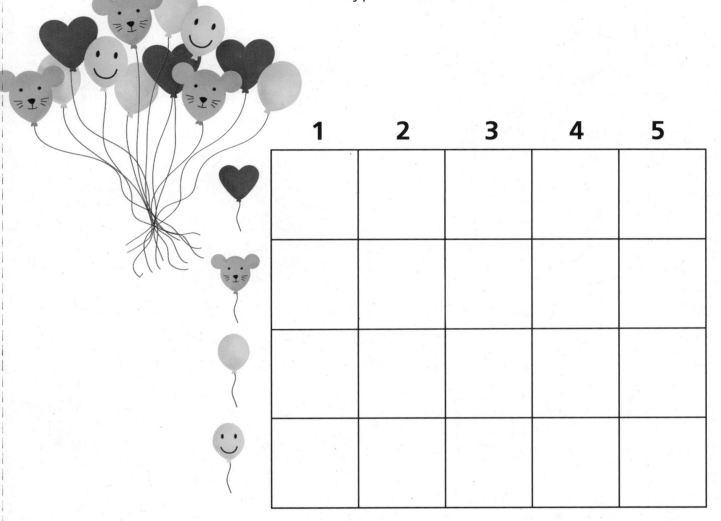

|   | 1 | 2 | 3 | 4 | 5 |
|---|---|---|---|---|---|

**1.** Which has the highest number?

**2.** Which has the lowest number?

**3.** Which balloons have the same number?

# LONG VOWEL O

Circle or fill in the letters that make the **long o** sound.

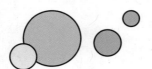

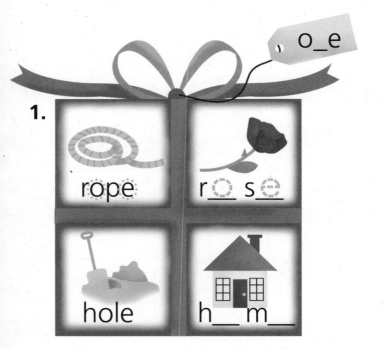

o_e

**1.**

rope

r○ s⊖

hole

h__ m__

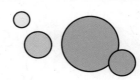

oe

**2.**

doe

t__ __

Joe

h__ __

oa

**3.**

loaf

b__ __t

goat

t__ __d

ow

**4.**

row

b__ __

tow

m__ __

# DIME TIME

Look at the price for each item.
Draw a line to the group of dimes that matches the price.

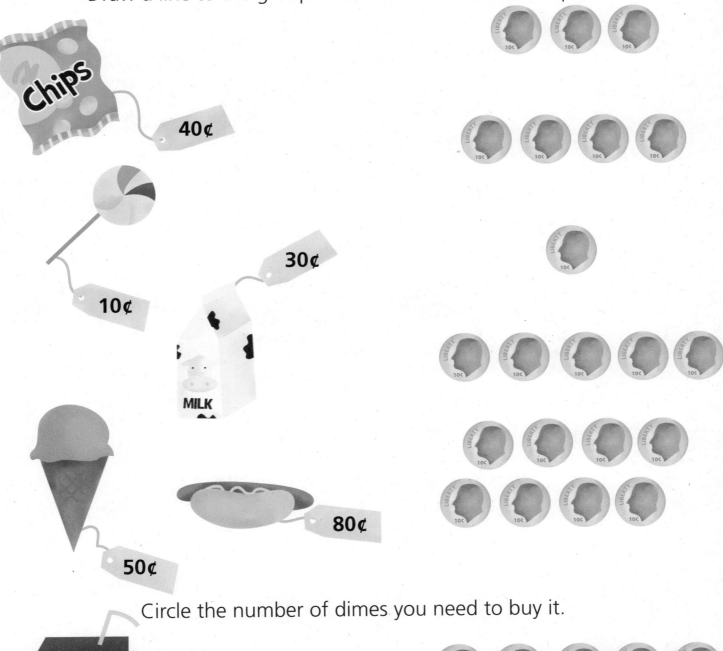

**Chips** 40¢

30¢

10¢

**MILK**

80¢

50¢

Circle the number of dimes you need to buy it.

100% Juice 70¢

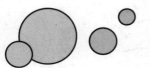

# LONG VOWEL U

Fill in the letters that make the **long u** sound.

**1.**

**u_e**

t__b___    t___n___    m___l___    J___n___

**2.**

**ue**

gl___ ___    S___ ___    bl___ ___    d___ ___

Review all the vowel pairs with **silent e**.
Write the name of each picture.

**3.**

**a_e**
**i_e**
**o_e**
**u_e**

_____    _____    _____    _____

# TWO BY TWO TRAINS

Count by 2s and write the missing numbers.

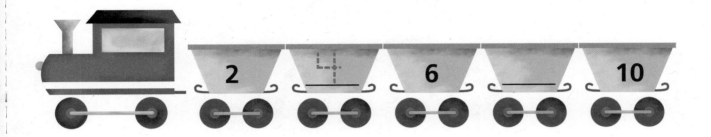

2    4    6    ___    10

2   4   ___   ___   10   ___   14   ___   18   20

Circle the train with numbers that count by 2s.

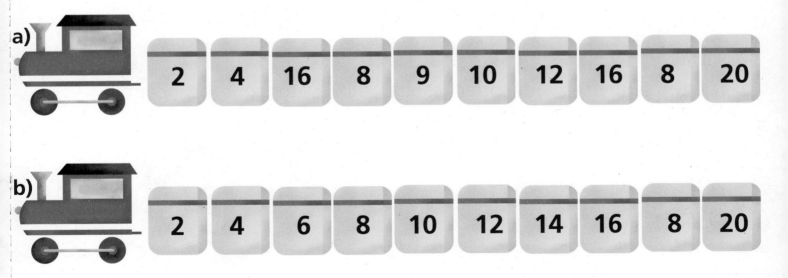

a) 2   4   16   8   9   10   12   16   8   20

b) 2   4   6   8   10   12   14   16   8   20

# CAPITAL COMPETITION

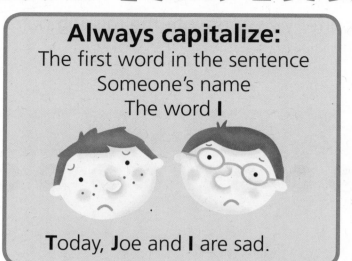

**Always capitalize:**
The first word in the sentence
Someone's name
The word **I**

**T**oday, **J**oe and **I** are sad.

Circle the capital letters in each group of sentences. Count the capital letters and see which group has the highest number.

**1.** Five kids ride the bus. Six kids ride bikes. Joe rides in a car. I like Joe. Today I ride with Joe.

_____

**2.** I have a dog. His name is Max. I put Max in the tub. My dog Max gives me a hug. Max and I have fun.

_____

Circle the sentences with correct capitalization. Cross out the incorrect sentences.

**3.** Joe and i ride the bus.

**4.** Max is a dog.

**5.** I ride my bike with Joe.

**6.** the tub is for Max.

# INCHING ALONG

Measure each object. Write the number of inches.

**1.**

_____ inches

**2.** CRAYON

_____ inches

**3.** _____ inches

**4.**

_____ inches

# THE LONG RACE

Circle the word that names each picture.
Each time you hear a long vowel sound, that vowel scores a point.
See which vowel wins the race!

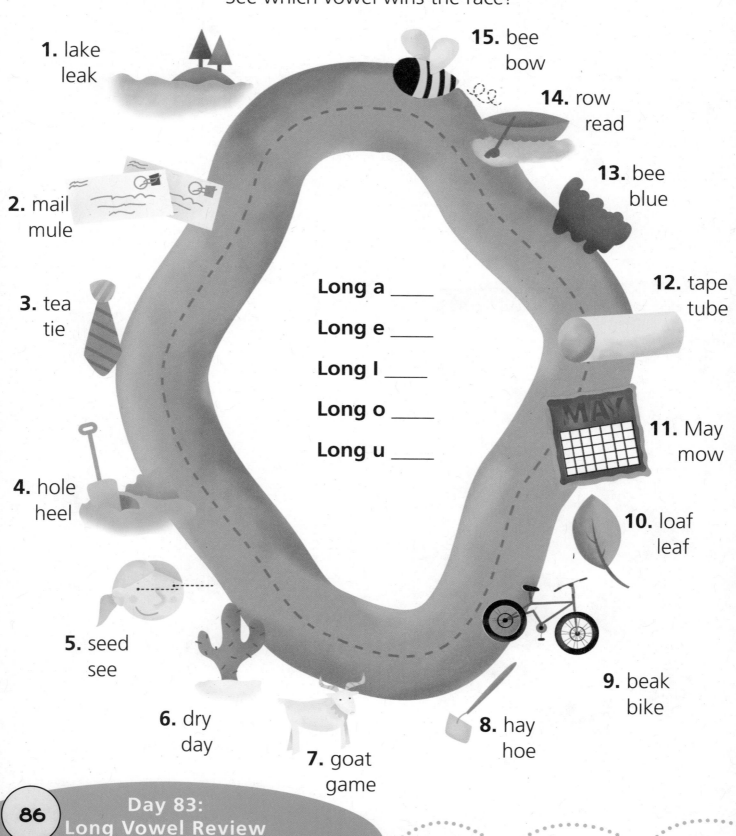

1. lake
   leak

2. mail
   mule

3. tea
   tie

4. hole
   heel

5. seed
   see

6. dry
   day

7. goat
   game

8. hay
   hoe

9. beak
   bike

10. loaf
    leaf

11. May
    mow

12. tape
    tube

13. bee
    blue

14. row
    read

15. bee
    bow

Long a _____

Long e _____

Long I _____

Long o _____

Long u _____

# GARDEN GRAPH

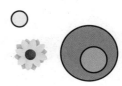

| | | | | | |
|---|---|---|---|---|---|
| 10 | | | | | |
| 9 | | | | | |
| 8 | ▓ | | | | |
| 7 | ▓ | | | | |
| 6 | ▓ | | | | |
| 5 | ▓ | | | | |
| 4 | ▓ | ▓ | | | |
| 3 | ▓ | ▓ | | | |
| 2 | ▓ | ▓ | ▓ | | |
| 1 | ▓ | ▓ | ▓ | | |

Read the sentences and complete the graph.

There are 6  in the garden.

There are 3  in the garden.

Now use the graph to solve the problems.

**1.** How many  ? _____   **2.** How many  ? _____

**3.**  +  = _____   **4.**  + 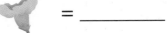 = _____

**5.**  –  = _____   **6.**  –  = _____

# SILLY SENTENCES

Draw a line from each sentence to its matching picture.

**1.** A fly is on the pie.

**2.** The queen is in jeans.

**3.** The glue is blue.

**4.** The mail is in the pail.

**5.** The goat is on a boat.

**a)**

**b)**

**c)**

**d)**

**e)**

**Day 85:**
**Sentence Decoding**

# GREATER OR LESS?

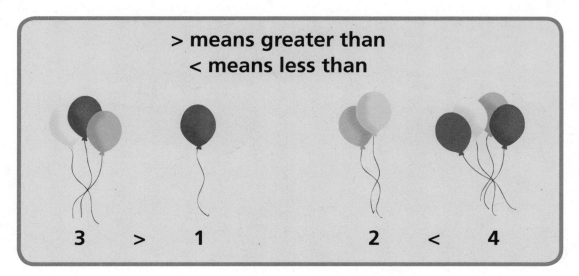

> means greater than
< means less than

3 > 1          2 < 4

Fill in > or <.

**1.** 3 _____ 10

**2.** 8 _____ 4

**3.** 15 _____ 5

**4.** 3 _____ 13

**5.** 20 _____ 2

**6.** 32 _____ 23

**7.** 40 _____ 50

**8.** 16 _____ 61

**9.** 7 _____ 77

**10.** 80 _____ 58

**11.** 69 _____ 99

**12.** 100 _____ 10

# LONG AND SHORT SORT

Draw a line from each picture to the short or the long vowel box.

**Short Vowels**

**Long Vowels**

Day 87:
Compare Vowels

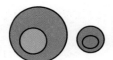

# COIN COUNT

Match the groups of coins that equal the same amount.

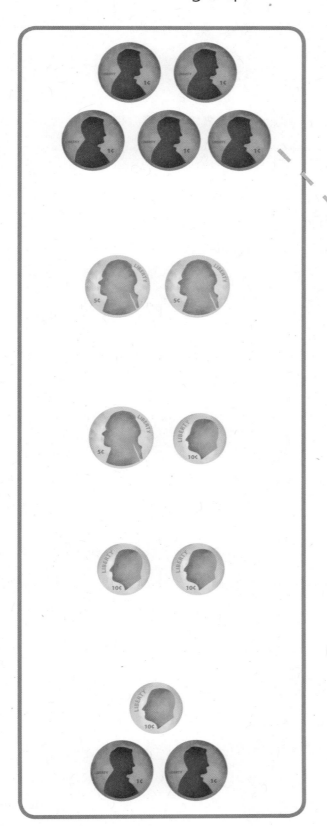

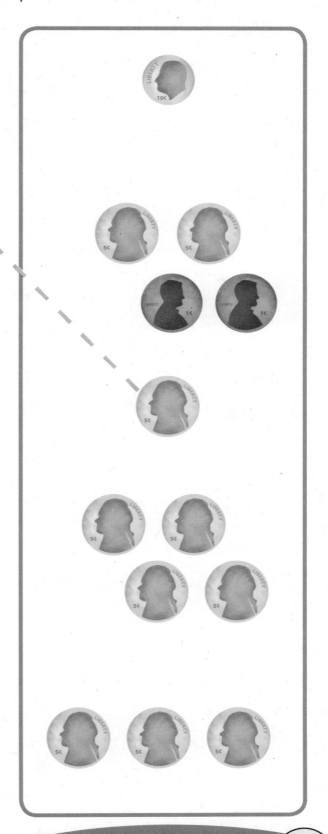

# END GAME

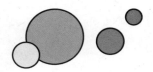
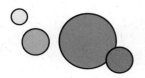

| Use a  .  to end a statement. | **You are Joe.** |
| Use a  ?  to end a question. | **Are you Joe?** |
| Use a  !  to add emphasis. | **You are not Joe!** |

Circle the punctuation at the end of each sentence. Count how many of each kind. See which mark has the highest number.

Max has a box. What is in the box? Is it a sock? No, it's not a sock. Is it a cap? No, it's not a cap. Open the box, Max! What do you see? It's a pie!

| . | ? | ! |
| --- | --- | --- |
| ___ | ___ | ___ |

Read each sentence. Add a period or a question mark.

**1.** Why are you sad

**2.** You are in the tub

**3.** The bug is on the rug

**4.** Are you in the car

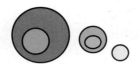 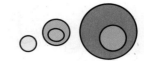

**3:00**

**3:30**

To show time to the half hour, the big hand is on the 6. The little hand is halfway between two numbers.

## Circle the correct time.

1.

**4:00**
**4:30**

2.

**8:00**
**8:30**

3.

**10:00**
**10:30**

## Draw the hands on each clock.

**2:30**

**7:30**

**11:30**

# ANSWER KEY

**Page 4**

Bb    Bb    ___

Bb    ___    Bb

**Page 5**

**Page 6**

**Page 7**

**Page 8**

**Page 9**
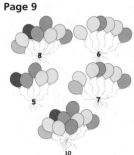

8    6

5    7

10

**Page 10**
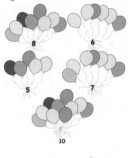

A B C D
E F G H I J
K L M N O P
Q R S T U
V W X
Y Z

a b c d e
f g h i j k
l m n o p q
r s t u v w
x y z

**Page 11**

S H A P E

**Page 12**
ant
cap
bag
rat

**Page 13**

**Page 14**
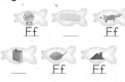

Ff    ___    Ff

___    Ff    Ff

**Page 15**
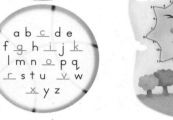

**Page 16**

**Page 17**

**Page 18**

**Page 19**

**Page 20**

**Page 21**
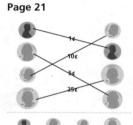

1¢    5¢    10¢    25¢

**Page 22**
hen
bell
egg
net

**Page 23**

**Page 24**

**Page 25**

**Page 26**

Kk    Kk

___    Kk    Kk    ___

**Page 27**

**Page 28**

**Page 29**

## Page 30

| | | |
|---|---|---|
| The cat likes Dad. ⑤ | A jar is in the bag. ② | Dad has a bag ① |
| Jam is on Dad. ⑥ | The cat likes jam, too. ④ | Dad likes jam. ③ |

## Page 31

11
12
13
14
15

11
12
13
14
15

## Page 32

hill
dig
pig
kid

## Page 33

## Page 34

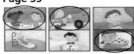

## Page 35

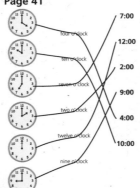

30 seconds   30 minutes

4 minutes   4 hours

1 minute   2 seconds

## Page 36

Nn   Nn

Nn   Nn

## Page 37

| ⑤ | 5¢ |
|---|---|
| ③ | 3¢ |
| ⑧ | 8¢ |
| ⑫ | 12¢ |

| 4¢ | |
|---|---|
| 7¢ | |
| 5¢ | |

## Page 38

## Page 39

1. $7 - 1 = 6$
2. $9 - 1 = 8$
3. $4 - 1 = 3$
4. $6 - 1 = 5$
5. $2 - 2 = 0$
6. $3 - 3 = 0$

## Page 40

2. Do not come. We are not ready.
3. What's in the box? You are not in the box.
4. We are not in that box. Look where we are.
5. Go look in the box. Now we can go hide.

## Page 41

four o'clock
ten o'clock
seven o'clock
two o'clock
twelve o'clock
nine o'clock

7:00
12:00
2:00
9:00
4:00
10:00

## Page 42

sock
pot
Bob
mop

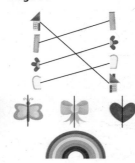

## Page 43

$4 + 2 = 6$
$3 + 2 = 5$
$5 + 3 = 8$
$2 + 5 = 7$
$3 + 3 = 6$

## Page 44

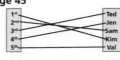

## Page 45

| 1st | Ted |
| 2nd | Jen |
| 3rd | Sam |
| 4th | Kim |
| 5th | Val |

Ted: third
Jen: fourth
Sam: second
Val: fifth
Kim: first

## Page 46

Rr   Rr

Rr   Rr

## Page 47

| $5-3 = 2$ | | | | | | | |
| $7-4 = 3$ | | | | | | | |
| $6-2 = 4$ | | | | | | | |
| $4-1 = 3$ | | | | | | | |
| $3-0 = 3$ | | | | | | | |
| $8-6 = 2$ | | | | | | | |
| $2-1 = 1$ | | | | | | | |
| $5-5 = 0$ | | | | | | | |
| $10-4 = 6$ | | | | | | | |

## Page 48

Beginning S   Ending S

## Page 49

1. $3 + 4 = 7$
2. $2 + 2 = 4$
3. $5 + 4 = 9$
4. $6 - 2 = 4$
5. $8 - 3 = 5$
6. $10 - 3 = 7$

## Page 50

1. football
2. doghouse
3. mailbox
4. anthill
5. gumball

## Page 51

## Page 52

gum
bus
bug
sun

## Page 53

2. $5 + 3 = 8$
3. $4 + 0 = 4$
4. $3 + 2; 4 + 1; 5 + 0$
5. $2 + 5; 6 + 1; 3 + 4$

## Page 54

Beginning T   10   Tt   Tt

Tt   Tt   Ending T

## Page 55

## Page 56

Beginning V

Beginning W

## Page 57

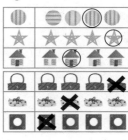

## Page 58

## Page 59

1. 9
2. 2
3. 5
4. 2
5. 7
6. 1
7. 9
8. 0
9. 10
10. 15
11. 8
12. 1

## Page 60

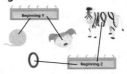

Beginning Y

Beginning Z

## Page 61

$3 + 3 = 6$
$4 - 2 = 2$
$1 + 8 = 9$
$7 - 2 = 5$
$3 + 5 = 8$
$6 - 3 = 3$

$3 - 0 = 3$
$8 + 0 = 8$
$8 - 6 = 2$
$6 + 3 = 9$
$10 - 4 = 6$
$4 + 1 = 5$

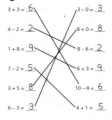

## Page 62

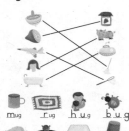

m̲ug   r̲ug   h̲ug   b̲ug

r̲at   b̲at   m̲at   h̲at

## Page 63

These missing numbers should be filled in:
1. 15; 25
2. 35; 45
3. 5; 15; 20
4. 30; 40; 50

## Page 64

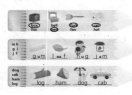

## Page 65

1. June
2. This question is answered when the days of the week are circled on the calendar.
3. 7
4. This question is answered when there is a star drawn on June 30.
5. 4
Bonus Question:
Answers will vary.

## Page 66

## Page 67

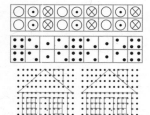

## Page 68

2. keys
3. car; cars
4. doll; dolls
5. box; boxes
6. bus; buses

## Page 69

## Page 70

1. b
2. c

## Page 71

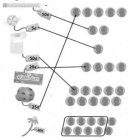

## Page 72

1. net       8. pot
2. pin       9. top
3. cap      10. dad
4. bug     11. jet
5. log     12. sun
6. egg     13. gas
7. king    14. sad
short a: 4 tally marks
short e: 3 tally marks
short i: 2 tally marks
short o: 3 tally marks
short u: 2 tally marks

## Page 73

1. d
2. a
3. c
4. b

10:00   2:00   4:00
7:00   12:00

## Page 74

1. lake; vase; game; tape
2. pail; rain; mail; maid
3. say; hay; May; pay

## Page 75

## Page 76

1. read; seal; jeans; ear
2. queen; heel; see; feet
3. leaf; tea; leak; beak
4. bee; jeep; tree; seed

## Page 77

10; 20; 30; 40; 50; 60; 70;
80; 90; 100

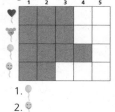
= 40
= 60
= 20

## Page 78

1. bike; nine; dime; five
2. tie; pie
3. fly; cry; sky; dry

## Page 79

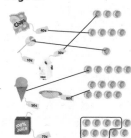
1.
2.
3.

## Page 80

1. rope; rose; hole; home
2. doe; toe; Joe; hoe
3. loaf; boat; goat; toad
4. row; bow; tow; mow

## Page 81

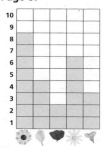

## Page 82

1. tube; tune; mule; June
2. glue; Sue; blue; due
3. lake; nine; rose; tube

## Page 83

Train b should be circled.

## Page 84

1. 8
2. 9
3. Joe and i ride the bus.
4. Max is a dog
5. I ride my bike with Joe.
6. the tube is for Max.

## Page 85

1. 2
2. 4
3. 1
4. 6

## Page 86

1. lake       9. bike
2. mail     10. leaf
3. tie       11. May
4. hole     12. tube
5. see      13. blue
6. dry      14. row
7. goat     15. bee
8. hoe
long a: 3 tally marks
long e: 3 tally marks
long i: 3 tally marks
long o: 4 tally marks
long u: 2 tally marks

## Page 87

1. 4
2. 8
3. 10
4. 11
5. 10
6. 8

## Page 88

1. b
2. d
3. a
4. c
5. e

## Page 89

1. 3 < 10
2. 8 > 4
3. 15 > 5
4. 3 < 13
5. 20 > 2
6. 32 > 23
7. 40 < 50
8. 16 < 61
9. 7 < 77
10. 80 > 58
11. 69 < 99
12. 100 > 10

## Page 90

## Page 91

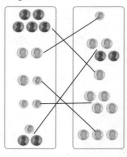

## Page 92

Max has a box. What is in the box? Is it a sock? No, it's not a sock. Is it a cap? No, it's not a cap. Open the box, Max!
What do you see? It's a pie!

3    4    2

1. Why are you sad ?
2. You are in the tub.
3. The bug is on the rug.
4. Are you in the car?

## Page 93

1. 4:30
2. 8:00
3. 10:30

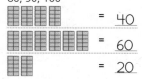